1-11-11

John,

you are a great father.
I thought of this book for
you to get Kalin closer to
your love of cars.

She talks all the time
about how she enjoys
bike riding when you
take her.

Salvador
LeBarn

Pebble® Plus

Rev It Up!

MUSCLE CARS

by Sarah Bridges, PhD

Consulting Editor: Gail Saunders-Smith, PhD

Consultant: Leslie Kendall, Curator
Petersen Automotive Museum, Los Angeles

CAPSTONE PRESS
a capstone imprint

Pebble Plus is published by Capstone Press,
151 Good Counsel Drive, P.O. Box 669, Mankato, Minnesota 56002.
www.capstonepub.com

 Books published by Capstone Press are manufactured with paper
containing at least 10 percent post-consumer waste.

Library of Congress Cataloging-in-Publication Data
Bridges, Sarah.
  Muscle cars / by Sarah Bridges.
    p. cm.—(Pebble plus. Rev it up!)
  Includes bibliographical references and index.
  Summary: "Simple text and full-color photographs briefly describe the history and unique features of muscle cars"—
Provided by publisher.
  ISBN 978-1-4296-5316-9 (library binding)
  1. Muscle cars—Juvenile literature. I. Title. II. Series.
  TL147.B75 2011
  629.222—dc22   2010025024

Editorial Credits
Erika L. Shores, editor; Ted Williams, designer; Laura Manthe, production specialist

Photo Credits
Alamy/Maksymenko 1, 15; Motoring Picture Library, 11 (top right); Nathan Luke, 9; Performance Image, 17, 19;
    TRANSTOCK/Guy Spangenberg, 13; Wes Allison, 21
Corbis/Seattle Post-Intelligencer Collection/Museum of History and Industry, 7
Dreamstime/Brad Sauter, 1; Raytags, 11 (bottom); Snehitdesign, 5
Kimball Stock/Ron Kimball, cover
Shutterstock/pasphotography, 11 (top left)

Artistic Effects
Shutterstock/Alexander Chaikin, archana bhartia, argus, fotoluminate

The author thanks Dale Nielsen and Dick Penk for their assistance on this book.

Note to Parents and Teachers

The Rev It Up! series supports national social studies standards related to science, technology,
and society. This book describes and illustrates muscle cars. The images support early readers
in understanding the text. The repetition of words and phrases helps early readers learn new
words. This book also introduces early readers to subject-specific vocabulary words, which are
defined in the Glossary section. Early readers may need assistance to read some words and to
use the Table of Contents, Glossary, Read More, Internet Sites, and Index sections of the book.

Printed in the United States of America in North Mankato, Minnesota.

092010   005933CGS11

Table of Contents

Mighty Cars. 4

Muscle Car History 6

Parts of a Muscle Car. 12

Rev It Up! 20

Glossary 22

Read More 23

Internet Sites. 23

Index 24

Mighty Cars

Muscle cars are built

to look strong and go fast.

Underneath a long hood

sits a roaring engine.

Vroom! Vroom!

Muscle Car History

In the 1950s, drivers fixed up
old cars into fast, flashy hot rods.
But some people wanted
speedy cars without doing
the work themselves.

Rev It Up!

Fans still drive early muscle cars.

Carmakers also sell new ones.

Drivers love the engine's roar

as they hit the gas and rev it up!

Glossary

engine—a machine in which fuel burns to provide power to move something

exhaust—the waste gases made by the engine

hood—the part of the car that opens and closes and usually covers the engine

horsepower—a unit for measuring an engine's power

hot rod—an old car or truck that has been fixed up so that it goes faster and looks cooler

muffler—a part on a car that lessens the noise of the engine; muscle car mufflers allow exhaust to move more freely, causing more noise to escape

Read More

Bailey, Katharine. *Muscle Cars.* Automania! New York: Crabtree Pub., 2007.

Poolos, J. *Wild about Muscle Cars.* Wild Rides. New York: PowerKids Press/Rosen Pub., 2008.

Internet Sites

FactHound offers a safe, fun way to find Internet sites related to this book. All of the sites on FactHound have been researched by our staff.

Here's all you do:

Visit *www.facthound.com*

Type in this code: 9781429653169

Super-cool stuff! Check out projects, games and lots more at **www.capstonekids.com**

Index

carmakers, 8, 20

Dodge Chargers, 10

engines, 4, 12, 14,
    16, 20

exhaust pipes, 16

Ford Mustangs, 10

hoods, 4

hood scoops, 14

horsepower, 12

hot rods, 6

mufflers, 16

noise, 16, 20

Pontiac GTOs, 10

sports cars, 8

stripes, 18

Word Count: 201

Grade: 1

Early-Intervention Level: 18